SUPER CUTE!

Baby Penguins

by Kari Schuetz

BLASTOFF! READERS

BELLWETHER MEDIA • MINNEAPOLIS, MN

Note to Librarians, Teachers, and Parents:

Blastoff! Readers are carefully developed by literacy experts and combine standards-based content with developmentally appropriate text.

Level 1 provides the most support through repetition of high-frequency words, light text, predictable sentence patterns, and strong visual support.

Level 2 offers early readers a bit more challenge through varied simple sentences, increased text load, and less repetition of high-frequency words.

Level 3 advances early-fluent readers toward fluency through increased text and concept load, less reliance on visuals, longer sentences, and more literary language.

Level 4 builds reading stamina by providing more text per page, increased use of punctuation, greater variation in sentence patterns, and increasingly challenging vocabulary.

Level 5 encourages children to move from "learning to read" to "reading to learn" by providing even more text, varied writing styles, and less familiar topics.

Whichever book is right for your reader, Blastoff! Readers are the perfect books to build confidence and encourage a love of reading that will last a lifetime!

This edition first published in 2014 by Bellwether Media, Inc.

No part of this publication may be reproduced in whole or in part without written permission of the publisher. For information regarding permission, write to Bellwether Media, Inc., Attention: Permissions Department, 5357 Penn Avenue South, Minneapolis, MN 55419.

Library of Congress Cataloging-in-Publication Data

Schuetz, Kari.
 Baby penguins / by Kari Schuetz.
   p. cm. – (Blastoff! readers. Super cute!)
 Audience: K to grade 3.
 Summary: "Developed by literacy experts for students in kindergarten through grade three, this book introduces baby penguins to young readers through leveled text and related photos"– Provided by publisher.
 Includes bibliographical references and index.
 ISBN 978-1-60014-931-3 (hardcover : alk. paper)
 1. Penguins–Infancy–Juvenile literature. I. Title.
 QL696.S47S38 2014
 598.47'139–dc23
                                                    2013003493

Printed in the United States of America, North Mankato, MN.

Table of Contents

Penguin Chick!

A baby penguin is called a chick. It starts life inside an egg.

egg

The chick **hatches** from the egg. It is covered in **down feathers**.

Mom and Dad

Mom and dad both care for the young chick. They are a team.

The chick stays with dad while mom hunts for fish. It is warm in his **brood pouch**.

brood pouch

Mom returns with food for the chick. She puts it in the chick's **beak**.

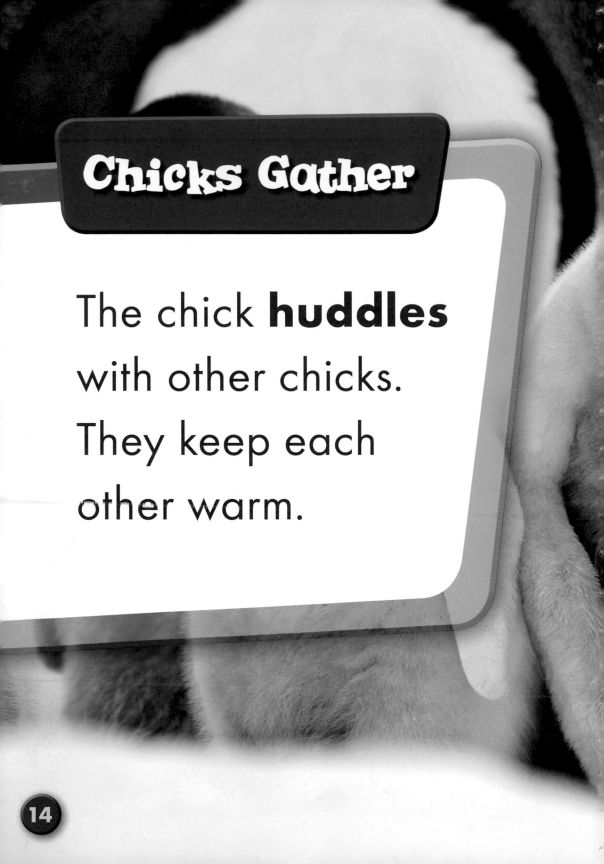

Chicks Gather

The chick **huddles** with other chicks. They keep each other warm.

The chick cannot fly. It still stretches its wings.

Soon the chick leaves mom and dad. It **waddles** across the ice.

Sometimes it slides on its belly. What fun!

Glossary

beak—the mouth of a bird

brood pouch—the pocket of feathered skin on the belly of a penguin; the brood pouch keeps a chick warm.

down feathers—soft feathers that keep birds warm

hatches—breaks out of an egg

huddles—gathers in a tight circle

waddles—moves like a duck

To Learn More

AT THE LIBRARY

Jeffers, Oliver. *Up and Down*. New York, N.Y.: Philomel Books, 2010.

Kawa, Katie. *Baby Penguins*. New York, N.Y.: Gareth Stevens Pub., 2012.

Rustad, Martha E. H. *A Baby Penguin Story*. Mankato, Minn.: Capstone Press, 2012.

ON THE WEB

Learning more about penguins is as easy as 1, 2, 3.

1. Go to www.factsurfer.com.

2. Enter "penguins" into the search box.

3. Click the "Surf" button and you will see a list of related Web sites.

With factsurfer.com, finding more information is just a click away.

Index